ESSE[NTIAL]
LONE PARENT SURVIVAL GUIDE

SUE SLIPMAN

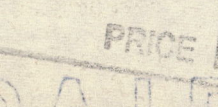

Published by
Boatswain Press Ltd
Dudley House, 12 North Street
Emsworth, Hampshire PO10 7DQ

© Sue Slipman 1993

The right of Sue Slipman to be identified as the author of this work has been asserted in accordance with the Copyright, Designs and Patents Act 1988

All rights reserved. No part of this publication may be reproduced, stored in a retrieval system, or transmitted in any form or by any means, electronic, mechanical, photocopying, recording or otherwise, without the prior permission of the copyright owner

Cover design, Slatter Anderson
Illustrations by Teri Gower
Printed in Great Britain

British Library Cataloguing-in-Publication Data
A catalogue record for this book is available from the British Library
ISBN 1 873432 34 8

ESSENTIAL LONE PARENT SURVIVAL GUIDE

Contents

Introduction	5
Routes into lone parenthood – problems to overcome	7
What happens when you get a divorce	12
Using the law in special circumstances	24
What will happen to the children	30
Money, benefits and taxation	37
Child Maintenance and the Child Support Agency	52
Housing and homelessness – keeping a roof over your heads	58
Getting back to work	69
Leisure and holidays	82
Useful organisations	94

INTRODUCTION

There are many routes into one parent family life, and nearly all of them are difficult to face. The majority of lone parents are married women who have gone through divorce, separation or bereavement. But there are mothers who have never married who may have been living with a partner. In the UK there are now over 1.1 million one parent families, with 1.9 million children. Nine out of ten lone parents are women. Men who become lone parents tend to have older children and do not face the same difficulties in needing childcare, and are often able to continue to work, but they have their own difficulties to face.

As well as parents who have permanently separated from partners, there are a range of other situations that make some parents virtually lone parents, such as a spouse in prison or serving away in the Armed Services.

However you become a lone parent, bringing up children alone is a demanding job. You have to learn to cope with the emotional demands of your children and become the only breadwinner in the family. Your family income is likely to drop dramatically and, as well as trying to make ends meet financially, you can experience a range of practical problems with housing and other crucial matters.

Lone parents are still often discussed in public as if they were social outcasts. These attitudes are gradually changing as now nearly every family has a member who is bringing up children alone. So, people are learning from personal experience that lone parents are mostly ordinary people doing a

very good job in difficult circumstances.
If you are a lone parent, don't panic! You can get help with the practical problems you face, and there are organisations that can offer social support, too, if you need it.

- *First you have to adjust to being a parent on your own*
- *Second you have to get your life back on track*

This book will take you through the initial stages of survival from the practical to the emotional. It will go on to point you in the direction of getting your life back on track and seeking training and work opportunities for yourself, and childcare support for your children.

ROUTES INTO LONE PARENTHOOD – PROBLEMS TO OVERCOME

Whatever route you take into lone parenthood you will share some common problems with those who took a different path to get there.

Separation and divorce

The majority of one parent families are created as a result of separation and divorce, and this route into lone parenthood can be very fraught. You and your children may have experienced a good deal of pain in a separation from your ex-partner and you may be trying to overcome bitterness in order to set up a positive relationship for the sake of the children. This can be very difficult.

Few experiences of a relationship breakdown are easy, unless both partners want to separate and are very mature about their reasons for doing so. If you are being left with the children while he or she goes off with a new partner there is bound to be enormous anger and sense of betrayal. If you are taking the children away from your partner, they will feel distraught and may feel like taking revenge.

Often when the decision is made to separate, it breaks the well-spring of emotions that has been deliberately held back as you have tried to make the relationship work.

In these circumstances it is very hard not to use the children as a kind of battleground over which you fight to prove which one of you is in the right. We do know that such parental fighting does a great deal of harm to children. Some of it is long term and may affect their health and their prospects for success and, in many cases, the harm is already done by the time parents decide to separate.

Becoming a lone parent through bereavement

Experiencing the death of a partner, even where it is expected as a result of illness, carries with it the most enormous trauma and adjustment. If the relationship was a loving and positive one then the sense of loss and grief can feel unbearable. But the emotions unleashed are unlikely to be straightforward. They can range through shock, denial, anger, anxiety and guilt.

Long-term relationships build many layers of interdependency. Many of these layers will have been warm and comforting, but some may be full of resentment for areas of life in which the partners have felt restricted by the arrangements between them. One partner may have made more of the sacrifices for the family than the other. So, in the initial phase mixed in with the shock of death and sense of grief will be a range of responses which may make the surviving partner feel deeply ashamed.

Couples often take on useful emotional functions for each other. Or they compensate for each other's inadequacies – if he is irritable, she will be serene and calm. When a partner dies, the surviving partner has to reclaim bits of their own personality. This can make them feel deeply insecure about who they are and there may be a lot of painful re-learning to do about themselves.

The most common response is anger that your partner has left you to cope with all this by yourself. This is particularly the case for women who have been dependent during their relationship and let their partner sort out all the practical and money matters and make all the decisions. It can be even worse where the surviving partner has not kept any friendships that are independent of the marriage, because all too often newly bereaved people discover that joint friendships do not survive when they are on their own. This can mean a real narrowing down of your social life and that of your children.

Grieving can take a long time and must be allowed to run its course, but in our society it is seen as a very private matter. People are often embarrassed by grief that tends to go on 'too long'. Most people find it difficult to cope with the full emotional scope of other people's grief. So, after the funeral and the socially acceptable times to sympathise, you may find that people either tend to shun you, or treat you as if you have now, rightly, pulled yourself together. If you have the kind of friends you trust to just listen to your deepest anxieties and fears you should try to talk to them. But it can also be valuable to seek more professional help from experienced counsellors, such as those who work with Cruse - Bereavement Care. Some local authorities provide similar services and further information about available services can be obtained from your local CAB or the National Association of Bereavement Services.

Whatever the reaction of your friends, you will be making major adjustments in your life and expectations. If you can you should avoid making any really important decisions whilst you are in this phase of grief. There are many practical issues to be taken care of, but many of the longer term ones can wait. Some people do throw themselves into dealing with these tasks in order to give themselves a structure within which to cope. But you really should try to do the minimum that needs to be done, giving yourself time for reflection about what you really want for the longer term. If you make decisions at this phase you may do so in the shadow of what you think your former partner would have wanted, when the outcome of this phase of grieving ought to be to permit you to live your own life and make your own decisions based upon your needs and wishes.

On the positive side there is far more sympathy for widows and widowers in our society than for lone parents through any other route. So, you may not have to carry the social stigma that other lone parents face. You may also be financially better off if you qualify for either Widowed Mother's Allowance or Widow's Pension.

Having a child on your own

Lone parents who have children outside marriage have historically had the hardest time. But this group has so many different kinds of people in it. Most are women, but now some lone fathers end up holding the baby. Some are career women fearful of the ticking of the biological time clock who decide to go ahead and have a child. Women in this position are still a very small percentage of the total and they are often established in a well-paid job, can afford the costs of childcare, and have thought long and hard about what they are taking on and the change it will make to their lives.

Many more unmarried mothers are young and not established in careers. Some are very young. The shock of motherhood and the demands it makes can be very great for a young woman. Too often she thinks that the arrival of the baby will ensure that the boyfriend will stay with her and happy family life will result. All too often he cannot cope and disappears and the full weight of the responsibility falls upon a youngster who is ill-prepared to carry it. Many young mothers do very well, particularly where they have strong support from their own families, but they have first to learn the skills of parenting before they can think about the longer term financial independence of their family.

There is no longer any major legal discrimination between children born in and outside marriage. *The exception is for the child of unmarried parents. Where the child's mother is a foreign national and the child's father British, the child cannot inherit nationality from the father.* But there are some significant differences in rights between parents on the basis of marital status. Nevertheless the issues that confront lone parents are the same:

- *getting your benefits and tax sorted out*
- *seeking the payment of child maintenance*
- *sorting out the separation or divorce*
- *planning to go back to work*
- *planning for some leisure time and holidays*

ESSENTIAL

WHAT HAPPENS WHEN YOU GET A DIVORCE

Going through a divorce is a painful business. You may still be uncertain about whether or not you want to split up or divorce. If you want to find out what your position will be if you do split up you can see a solicitor to get advice. You may also want someone to talk to about how you are feeling either with or without your partner. In this case you may find it helpful to seek counselling. But you may already have been to seek help to see if you can rescue the relationship and resolve the problems between you and decided that, if reconciliation is impossible, separation is the only path you can take. However it happens, there will have been a lot of distress before the decision to separate and divorce was taken.

Now, apart from the pain and grief and anger which you may be feeling, there are all the practical things to sort out. You have to deal with the question of where you are both going to live, how you are going to divide up your property, what you are going to live on and arrangements for seeing the children. It can all seem impossibly complicated and frightening when you first start.

Do not expect too much of the law. Divorce law is not designed to punish either of you for past bad behaviour, or reward you for good behaviour. Only in extreme cases is behaviour taken into account when financial matters are sorted out. The law looks forward to what your life apart will be like and tries to achieve a working solution for both of you. You may well feel that the past is being ignored unfairly.

Using conciliation

Conciliation *(often called Mediation)* is different from reconciliation as it is not trying to help you and your partner to stay together. It takes place after you have decided finally to separate and it is a method of trying to reach agreement between partners about what is to happen when they separate and divorce. It is done by discussion and negotiation. One or two trained workers sit with you and try to help the discussion take a constructive form, sometimes acting a bit like umpires. Mostly the issues dealt with concern the children, but some services also offer to deal with financial negotiations. It can be much more satisfactory than trying to resolve issues by taking things to court. It can also be cheaper, most services charge per session, but often work out their fee according to your ability to pay.

There are a number of services round the country who offer sessions to divorcing or separating couples. Your solicitor may know about the local services, and the County Court and Citizens Advice Bureaux may also have details. You can also contact the organisations listed at the end of this book.

Conciliation is probably best tried at an early stage, before problems have become too great, or things have got very bitter between you and your spouse. You both need to be willing to try to reach an agreement, even if you have very different views about what that should be.

Conciliation is not a substitute for legal advice. You will still each need a solicitor to check any financial or other agreement you come to in order to ensure that it is fair and reasonable for each of you.

Acting for yourself

If you do not use a solicitor you will be described as acting 'in person' at the court. If you are to be the *'Petitioner'* (ie the person applying for divorce) you should go to your local County Court, checking first by telephone that it deals with divorce cases. In London this is the Principal Registry of the Family Division of the High Court at Somerset House, Strand, London WC2R 1LP. The divorce court staff will supply you with the forms that you need and will advise you about completing them. There are five free leaflets available at the court to help you. You can also telephone the Principal Registry in London on 071 936 6000 for the leaflets.

Seeing a solicitor

You do not need to see a solicitor, but it is sensible to do so even if you think that you are going to act for yourself afterwards. The reason is that, at a first interview, a solicitor will be able to outline for you the likely outcome of events. You can find out whether you will be granted a divorce, and what will probably happen about the children and money and property.

There are a number of reasons for seeing a solicitor. Apart from the obvious task of advising you about the law, a solicitor can help you decide between the various courses of action open to you.

If you want to start divorce proceedings your solicitor will do the paperwork. Solicitors can also act as an emotional screen between you and your spouse and help reduce the areas of conflict between you.

Finding a good solicitor

You will want to find a good solicitor and may not have a clue where to find a specialist in Family Law. The Solicitors Family Law Association (SFLA) is an association of solicitors, most of who do specialise in family law, who believe in trying to resolve matters wherever possible by agreement rather than by going to court. You can write to their secretary with a stamped addressed envelope at –

The Solicitors Family Law Association (SFLA)
PO Box 302 • Keston • Kent BR2 6EZ

You will be sent a list of the members of the SLFA in your area. *In an emergency you will be able to ask for the name if you telephone on 0689 850227.*

Local libraries and Citizens Advice Bureaux keep lists of solicitors in their area *(Solicitors Regional Directories)* which show the types of work they do. These also list which solicitors offer the Legal Aid scheme which helps to pay for legal costs.

Friends or local one parent family groups, such as Gingerbread, may have first-hand experience of local solicitors. A solicitor may not advise both partners in a matrimonial dispute. It is good practice for a solicitor who has previously acted for you both to refuse to act for either of you and to refer you to separate solicitors.

Preparing for your visit to the solicitor

Before you go to see a solicitor for the first time you should prepare some bits of information to save time and costs: a note of the dates of birth of you and your spouse, and the children, and date when you married; any paperwork covering previous legal proceedings between you; a worked budget of what it costs to run your household; and a history of the most important events in your marriage, such as house purchases.

If you think you will want to start divorce proceedings you should take your marriage certificate – the official copy, not a photocopy.

You may be able to get Legal Aid to cover your costs. At the first interview your solicitor will work out from your income and capital whether you come within the financial limits. If you get Income Support you will automatically qualify for full Legal Aid and will not have to make a financial contribution. For others there is a sliding scale of contributions based on the amount of your income.

You get Legal Aid by completing application forms which your solicitor sends off to the Legal Aid Board. The Board decides whether your case deserves Legal Aid (generally a formality) and how much you should pay as a contribution. Contributions are payable monthly for as long as the case lasts so the quicker the case is dealt with, the less you will have to pay. To accept the offer you sign the form and send off the first payment. If in doubt about this, speak to your solicitor. In some cases, Legal Aid can be granted on an emergency basis, and in extreme cases a claim can be authorised over the telephone. If you gain a lump sum of capital over £2,500 you will be expected to pay for the costs out of the excess. Any money over £2,500 which you are awarded (other than maintenance) can be used to pay off the Legal Aid bill. Likewise, any property you have may have a charge put on it so that when it is sold, your Legal Aid costs are paid to the Legal Aid Board.

Legal steps you can take

If you live apart from your spouse and you no longer regard yourself as married then you are separated as far as the Inland Revenue and the DSS are concerned, and will be treated as a 'single parent' by these bodies if you have the children living with you. You do not need a legal document to confirm your status.

You and your spouse can set out the financial terms on which you have separated, or intend to separate in a *'Deed of Separation'* which yor solicitor can help you draw up. This is a binding legal contract and you can go to court to enforce the promises which it contains, although this is not always straightforward. This Deed is not enforceable in later divorce proceedings as the court will not let you sign away your rights. In any divorce proceedings you must make sure all claims are dealt with by court order.

There is an order called a Judicial Separation which you can obtain from a Divorce Court. The procedure and the facts that have to be proved to obtain this Order are the same as a divorce except at the end there is no Decree Absolute, so you are not divorced, and neither party is free to marry again. These are sometimes applied for by people who have very strong religious beliefs against divorce as they allow for the same ability to make arrangements about property and children as divorces, but without finally ending the marriage. They are used more rarely now.

You have to have been married one year before you can start divorce proceedings. Your spouse will be called the *'Respondent'* if you are applying for the divorce – ie if you are the *'Petitioner'*. The sole ground for a divorce is that the marriage has broken down irretrievably, but this has to be proved by stating one of five *'facts'* to the court –

1. That the Respondent has committed adultery and that the Petitioner finds it intolerable to live with him/her.

2. That the Respondent has behaved in such a way that the Petitioner cannot reasonably be expected to live with him/her.

3. That the Respondent has *'deserted'* the Petitioner – ie left her/him without good reason and against her/his will – for a period of at least two years.

4. That the couple has been separated for two years with consent – often known as the *'no fault'* divorce.

5. That the couple has been separated for five years.

LONE PARENT SURVIVAL GUIDE

How the divorce law works

If you are acting for yourself as Petitioner you will be sent the same papers as the Petitioner's solicitors in this description and will have to take the same steps.

Where the divorce or judicial separation is unopposed – called *'undefended'* divorce – the normal procedure is as follows –

1. The Petitioner's solicitors prepare the papers. The court requires a Statement of Arrangements for the children to be completed and signed by the Petitioner. This tells the court what the present arrangements for the children are and whether these are settled for the future. Where possible this should be agreed by the Respondent before the petition is sent off to the court. The Petitioner's solicitors will send it out to the Respondent or his/her solicitors and ask him/her to send it back.

2. When the Statement of Arrangements is returned and the other papers are in order, the Petitioner's solicitors send the petition – *the legal document which sets out the reasons for the divorce* – and the Statement of Arrangements and the marriage certificate to the court where a case-file is opened and a number is allocated to it. If the Respondent does not agree the arrangements for the children the petition can still be filed.

3. The court sends the copy petition and Statement of Arrangements to the Respondent (and where appropriate the Co-respondent – this is the person with whom your husband/wife has committed adultery) together with a form of Acknowledgement of Service.

4 The Respondent – and Co-respondent where

appropriate – completes answers to the questions on the Acknowledgement of Service and sends it back to the court. The Respondent can also send his/her own Statement of Arrangements for the children at this point.

5. The court sends a photocopy of the Acknowledgement of service to the Petitioner's solicitors.

6. The Petitioner's solicitors prepare a written document called an Affidavit in support of the petition for the Petitioner to swear before another solicitor.

7. The Petitioner's solicitors send the sworn Affidavit to the court together with a request for directions for trial.

8. The judge reads the documents that have reached the court and, provided he/she is satisfied that the case has been made out, Decree Nisi can be pro-

nounced. Provided the Judge is also satisfied with the arrangements for the children, these too will be approved. The court then fixes the date and time for the pronouncement of Decree Nisi of divorce (or Judicial Separation). The court sends out the notice of the time and date to both Petitioner and Respondent or to their solicitors. If the Judge wants further details about the children, the court will either ask for more written evidence or fix an appointment for the parties to attend court.

9. Decree Nisi is formally pronounced in court. Generally, no attendance is necesary.

10. Six weeks and one day after Decree Nisi – provided the Judge is satisfied with the arrangements for any children – the Petitioner can apply for a Decree Absolute to be made, by sending a form to the court. If the Petitioner delays applying for more than three months after this date then the Respondent can apply, by requesting the court to fix an appointment to consider the matter. The Petitioner is notified of the appointment and can raise objections.

What the courts can do about money

On divorce the court has the power to adjust income and capital, and this is done in one or more of the following ways:

- *Maintenance – often called periodical payments – for a spouse.*
- *Lump sum orders for spouse and/or children.*
- *A transfer of property order to the husband/wife and/ or children. This is usually used when sorting out what will happen to the matrimonial home.*

Traditionally the Courts have also had the power to make maintenance orders for children. However,

ESSENTIAL

when the Child Support Act 1991 came into effect in April 1993, this power disappeared except in special circumstances. From April 1993, maintenance claims started to be taken over gradually – starting with new claimants for benefit – by the Child Support Agency. Therefore some maintenance claims will still be dealt with by the courts until April 1997 when the Child Support Agency is in a position to deal with all claims.

After the divorce
You should keep all the papers which you have had from your solicitor or the court safely. At the very least make sure that you have a copy of the Decree Absolute and the final financial order. In each case you need the top copy which the court sent with its stamp on it in ink, not just a photocopy.

USING THE LAW IN SPECIAL CIRCUMSTANCES

How to stop your spouse selling off property
Sometimes your spouse may try to sell your house or other valuable objects in order to hide the money if they think you are going to make a claim in the divorce settlement. If this is attempted you can apply to the court for an injunction to stop it happening. If it has already happened the court has powers to undo transactions so as to recover property. You will need some proof that it is likely to happen, or that your spouse has threatened to do this and is able to carry out these threats. The more information you have about their assets, the easier it is to freeze them in this way.

How to work out your household budget
When working out monthly figures remember that a month is 4.33 weeks not just 4.
If you have the bills to back up the figures take them with you to your solicitor.

Accommodation   (£ per month)
Mortgage/Rent

Endowment policy

Council tax

Water rates

Electricity

Gas

Telephone

Service Charge/Ground rent

Oil/Solid fuel (coal)

Household expenses (**£ per month**)
Food/housekeeping

House insurance

Contents insurance

Repairs/service contracts

Cleaner

TV licence

TV/Video hire

Other items *(please list)*

ESSENTIAL

Car (£ per month)
Insurance

Road tax

Maintenance

Petrol

Loan for purchase
(state when it will end)

Children (£ per month)
School expenses
(Remember to average out
term-time costs over the whole year)
Travel to school

School dinners

Uniforms

Outgoings and trips

School fees

Other school expenses *(please list)*

Private lessons *(please list)*

LONE PARENT SURVIVAL GUIDE

Out-of-school expenses   **(£ per month)**
Leisure activities *(ballet, football etc, please list)*

Clothes and shoes

Nappies

Doctor

Dentist

Optician

Childminder/nanny

Hairdressing

Books

Toys

Christmas/birthdays

Other items *(please list)*

ESSENTIAL

Your expenses (**£ per month**)
Clothes and shoes

Hairdressing

Doctor

Dentist

Optician

Prescription charges

Dry cleaning

Entertainment

Travel to work

Lunches at work

Holidays *(including children if appropriate)*

Subscriptions *(please list)*

Other items *(please list)*

Total £

Definitions of terms you may come across in divorce proceedings

- *Petitioner* – the person who applies for the divorce
- *Respondent* – the person who is being divorced
- *Co-respondent (in cases of adultery)* – the named person with whom the adultery was committed
- *Petition* – The legal document which sets out the reasons for the divorce
- *Statement of arrangements for the children* – a detailed form which tells the court where the children live and go to school and what the arrangements for contact are. Ideally both of you agree the wording. It is filed at the court at the same time as the Petition
- *Acknowledgement of service* – the official form which the Respondent *(and co-respondent)* completes and signs to show that she/he has received the Petition, and whether or not she/he intends to defend it
- *Affidavit in support of the petition* – a written statement which the Petitioner swears to confirming that the contents of the Petition are true and that she/he wants to proceed with the divorce
- *Request for directions for trial* – a form which asks the court to fix a date for Decree Nisi
- *Decree nisi* – the final decree of divorce. Once it is made the marriage is at an end and both parties may remarry if they wish to do so
- *Counsel* – another word for a barrister
- *Ancillary relief/Financial relief* – all the financial claims which either party may make in divorce proceedings.

WHAT WILL HAPPEN TO THE CHILDREN

Many parents are worried about the impact of living in a one parent family upon children, whether this occurs through bereavement, divorce and separation or birth outside marriage. Often the route into lone parenthood has been stressful and painful. It may be very difficult for parents who have been through major upheaval to reach sensible conclusions about arrangements for children.

Legal arrangements for children

The law about parental relationships with children post separation has changed dramatically over the past few years. Previously, parents could be awarded *'care and control'* and *'custody'*, and this was the bundle of rights that gave both authority over the child and sorted out the living arrangements. The Children Act 1989 turned the concept into one of parental responsibility which does not end with separation or divorce. It defines parental responsibility as – *All the rights, duties, powers and responsibilities and authority which by law a parent of a child has in relation to the child and his property.*

Parental responsibility is automatic for mothers, and married fathers. Unmarried fathers do not automatically have parental responsibility, but as a parent he has a duty to maintain his child and the child can still inherit through him. But he can acquire parental responsibility if he had a Custody Order under the old law, if the mother makes a *'Parental Responsibility Agreement'* with him, or if he applies to the court, proving that he is the child's father and the court judges that it is in the child's interest to give him a Parental Responsibility Order. In addition, if the court grants him a Residence Order for the child it must also make a Parental Responsibility Order simultaneously.

In general, the court will not make any specific orders unless an *'issue'* or disagreement arises between the parents. The Courts will assume that parents can make agreed arrangements for their own children. The Court's two guiding principles will be that the child's welfare is of paramount interest and that an order should only be made if that is better for the child than relying on informal arrangements. It must also take into account the child's wishes and feelings, physical, emotional and educational needs, the effect of a change in circumstances, the capability of the parents or other relevant people to meet these and any other relevant factor such as age, sex, background or other characteristics. If the need arises a range or orders can be made covering residence, contact, family assistance and orders covering specific issues or stopping one of the parents from taking a particular action.

When a case comes to court, the child's wishes will normally be heard by a welfare officer who will prepare a report with recommendations to the court.

What to do if your child is in danger of being abducted

There are a number of parents, particularly those who have had children with a foreign national, who worry about their child being abducted. There is nothing quite so agonising as having your children taken from you without permission after you think the whole grisly business is over – but it does happen in extreme cases.

If the children have been *'snatched'* and you know that they are still in this country and are unlikely to be taken abroad, tell your solicitor immediately so that steps can be taken – under the Children Act 1989 – to have them returned to you.

If you think that there is any likelihood of them being taken out of the country get in touch with your local police station immediately and explain the circumstances. They can carry out a *'port alert'* to notify all ports of the danger of the children being taken. The police will need a full description of each child and their abductor. Supply recent photographs if possible. Also tell your solicitor at once so that steps can be taken to obtain a court order, ordering them not to be removed from this country and to be returned to you.

If you are worried that this may happen in the future because of a foreign connection of your ex-partner or threats which have been made in the past, mention this to your solicitor at an early stage in the proceedings so that you can consider whether safeguard measures can be taken.

Thankfully most children are not at risk of abduction, but enough parents have experienced the anguish of trying to find children who have already disappeared and it is better to take action immediately if you have any fears of this happening to your children.

Making arrangements between you

In general, couples facing relationship breakdown and divorce have more mundane if important arrangements to sort out, but they can also face difficulties in reaching agreement. There are independent conciliation services that can help divorcing or separating couples to sort out arrangements for children, particularly where there are communication difficulties. They normally deal with residence and contact issues. Some can help you reach financial agreement. Some courts make their own conciliation arrangements with the court welfare service, and some branches of *Relate* also offer services.

Helping the children to cope

When the arrangements for the children have been sorted out, attempting to maintain a relationship with your ex-partner is important. We know that almost 50% of divorced fathers lose contact with their children in the first year after divorce. This can be for a range of reasons, and it is obvious that behaviour within the relationship and towards its end may take a lot of getting over before the anger and bitterness has passed. Lots of parents do try to keep things civilised for the sake of the children, and many succeed, but an awful lot use their children as a kind of battleground over which to fight out the issues that lead to the break-up of the relationship. It should be equally obvious that in these circumstances the children are bound to suffer split loyalties and guilt. Children can take the blame for the break-up and internalise their guilt. Equally, if you deny access to the father they can see him as either the villain who damaged you or as the hero whose presence would have solved all the problems of their lives. If he disappears, they can feel rejected and unlovable. All these emotional responses are possible – none of them provide children with a sense of proportion or square with the reality of the individual.

It always seems far better to let the children experience their own judgement to eventually get things in proportion. The husband of a friend of mine, to whom she had been married for almost 20 years, announced one day that he was leaving her and their three children for another woman who was about to have his child. After the shock and the adjustment, they sorted out arrangements for their children whose attitude to him now is that they think he is a total wally, but they love him because he is 'Dad'.

Sometimes, because they mostly have more money than mothers, fathers can try to buy the affection of the children, thereby making the mother feel inadequate. It may be his inarticulate attempt to say sorry but it can seem like an unwelcome reminder to her of her poverty and his power. Such events can keep any bitterness brewing. In these circumstances your children may become adept at playing you off one against the other, to the longer term advantage of none of you.

If there has been a history of conflict between you, it is probably far better to have clear arrangements that you stick to. In time you may get a more relaxed relationship in which you can be flexible. A major lesson is to attempt to see the other person's point of view. You probably both feel like a victim of the situation and have some blame for the other partner, but you really do have to get over it for your children's sake. If you have been a genuine victim of cruelty or violence the courts may well not grant your ex-partner either a Parental Responsibility Order *(where you were not married)* or a Contact Order. They may well judge that it is not in the interests of your child to have contact with their father.

It is better, if it is at all possible, for the children to stay in the family home and continue at the same school. You may want a total break and to escape, but the children probably need as much stability as possible in as many areas as possible, given the other changes they need to adapt to.

Whatever the circumstances, it is important that the children are treated as people with rights and talked with about the situation. It is better if you can tell them of your impending split up together and reassure them that they will continue to be loved by both of you. They will have picked up the tension between you from a million tell-tale signs, and keeping them in the dark will only increase their worries and anxieties. You must also give them the opportunity to voice their wishes and desires and take these into account as far as possible. Children should not and cannot call all the shots, but they have the right to be heard and to have their feelings and views considered.

You might also want to discuss what is happening with their teachers at school. Often behaviour at school reveals a lot about what children are going through emotionally. It can also help avoid any public embarrassment for your children if adults in authority around them know what is going on and can make necessary allowances, or even offer the chance for a child who wants to talk to them.

MONEY, BENEFITS AND TAXATION

Your first problem will be to secure some income for you and the children. You may already work, but many lone parents will have given up work when they married. In any case you will probably not have enough money coming in regularly to keep the children and pay the bills. You need to know where and how to get extra income. Whilst the majority of lone parents want to work, they also need state assistance in getting a sufficient weekly income and will spend a period of time in receipt of various benefits. All the benefit rates quoted below apply from April 1993.

Social security benefits
Income support

If you are not working at all or working less than 16 hours per week, you will probably qualify for Income Support. This benefit is paid to people who have no or very low income. As a lone parent you must be over 16 to apply for it and have less than £8000.00 savings. Lone parents do not have to *'sign on'* as being available for work to claim Income Support. This benefit is means-tested so any income you already receive will be taken into account.

Income Support is paid through the Benefit Agency. It is important to keep the Benefit Agency informed of any change in your weekly income as this affects the amount you are entitled to receive. If you do not keep them informed you risk being asked to repay any benefit that has been 'overpaid'.

The benefit is made up of a number of elements as follows:

- **Personal Allowances** – *which depend upon your age and the age of your children*
- **Premiums** – *these depend on your particular circumstances*
- **Housing costs** – *covers mortgage interest for home owners, non-home owners get Housing Benefit*

These elements make up the 'applicable' amount. You must work this out, then calculate your income, and take your income away from the applicable amount in order to see what Income Support you will receive. Your income includes Child Benefit, maintenance, part-time earnings, most National Insurance Benefits, student loans or grants, money from lodgers or tenants although some of this is ignored, Statutory Sick Pay less tax on National Insurance and income you receive on capital. You are allowed to keep £15.00 of any money you earn after deductions for tax and National Insurance.

If you are a home owner, for the first 16 weeks you are on benefit half your mortgage interest will count as housing costs. After that, all the interest will count as housing costs. For details of Housing Benefit see page 43.

Any family receiving Income Support gets automatic help with Housing Benefit and Council Tax Benefit and receives the maximum amount of both, although you will still have to pay all your Water Rates from your Income Support. You also get free milk and vitamins if you are pregnant (and for any children under five years one month), free prescriptions and dental treatment and help with glasses and fares to hospital. You can apply to the Social Fund for a maternity payment and other help. Your

LONE PARENT SURVIVAL GUIDE

children can get free school meals and you may qualify for a uniform grant from the local authority.

Family Credit
Family Credit is a benefit for parents of any age who have at least one dependant child and are in low paid, full-time work of 16 or more hours. In order to

claim you must have savings of less than £8000. You make your claim by completing the form you get from the Benefits Agency and sending it off to:
Family Credit Unit
Government Buildings • *Warbeck Hill Road*
Blackpool FY2 0AX   *Telephone 0253 500050*
Claims are paid for a period of 26 weeks, so any change in your circumstances does not count during this period, but you must make a further claim every 26 weeks.

To calculate the amount of Family Credit you will receive there are four steps –
- *Calculate the maximum amount of Family Credit for someone in your circumstances*
- *Calculate your income*

See if you are above or below the 'threshold level' – currently £69.00.
- *If you are below threshold level you receive the maximum amount*
- *If you are above threshold level, you subtract the threshold level from your income, then deduct 70% of the resulting figure from the maximum Family Credit. The result is the Family Credit. The result is the Family Credit you will receive.*

In order to calculate the maximum Family Credit for your situation the following rates apply:

Personal allowances

Adult	£42.00
For each dependent child aged:	
18	£31.00
16-17	£22.20
11-15	£17.85
under 11	£10.75

To calculate your income add up any maintenance *(the first £15.00 does not count)*, earnings, money from lodgers or tenants *(some is ignored)*, and income on capital. But some income is completely ignored such as Chid Benefit and One Parent Benefit, Housing Benefit and things like Fostering Allowances. Earnings means the sum you receive after deductions for tax, national insurance and half of any pension contribution. Weekly earnings are calculated by taking the average of five weeks before the claim or two months if you are paid monthly. You will have to send pay slips off with your claim.

If you get Family Credit you are automatically entitled to apply for free prescriptions and dental treatment, help with glasses and a maternity payment from the Social Fund. In addition, whilst you are not automatically entitled, you may be able to claim Housing Benefit, Council Tax Benefit, milk and vitamins at a reduced price if you have a child under one, and clothing grants from the local education authority.

The Social Fund
The Social Fund is made up of three types of payment governed by rules about who qualifies and what amounts they will receive, and three types of payments that are discretionary. The 'regulatory' payments cover the Maternity Payment of £100 (claimable by those with less than £500 savings from 11 weeks before the child is born to 3 months after the birth – for those with more than £500 the amount reduces pound for pound), funeral payments and cold weather payments. There is no cash limit on this part of the Social Fund. People on Income

Support or Family Credit can claim the Maternity Payment and the Funeral Payment. People on Housing Benefit can claim the Funeral Payment. But only those on Income Support can claim the Cold Weather Payment and only in periods of very cold weather. If you think you should be eligible for one of these grants, but are refused it, you have the right to appeal to a tribunal.

There are three further types of payment which are paid at the discretion of the local Social Fund Officer from a cash limited fund. These payments include:

- *Community Care Grants*
- *Budgeting Loans*
- *Crisis Loans*

There is no statutory right to appeal if you are refused a payment under this part of the Social Fund.

People on Income Support can apply for a Community Care Grant for help in coming out of institutional or residential care, to avoid going into care, or to *'ease exceptional pressure'* on them or their families. Priority is given to people in stressful circumstances and for equipment such as cookers, heaters and start-up grants for furniture. The grant does not have to be repaid. Any savings up to £500 will be ignored but after that the sum you claim is reduced by a pound for every pound above the savings level. There is a minimum payment of £30 and, whilst there are no maximum payments as such, there are suggested maximums for certain items such as £500 plus £250 altogether for a grant.

You are more likely to get a Budgeting Loan than a

Community Care Grant, but it is always wise to apply for the grant first as you have to repay the loan through a deduction from you weekly Income Support at a rate of up to 15% of benefit. But at least Budgeting Loans are interest free – unlike private loans which work our far more expensive – often twice the amount borrowed, even though weekly repayments are less.

You can claim a Budgeting Loan if you have been on Income Support for 26 weeks and the same conditions apply as for Community Care Grants. The minimum payment is £30 and the maximum is £1000.00 less any loan you are already paying off. Priority is given to those items where refusal could cause hardship or risk to the health of anyone in the family such as beds, cookers or repairs to the home. Crisis Loans, which have to be repaid, are available to people aged over 16 to prevent risk of serious damage to health or safety. They are not limited to people on Income Support. If the loan is for living expenses the loan period will normally be over 14 days at 75% of the Income Support Personal Allowance rate and the under age 11 rate for any child.

Housing Benefit

Housing Benefit can be claimed by either private, Housing Association or council tenants who have less than £16,000.00 in savings or capital. Council tenants get a rent rebate and other tenants get a rent allowance. Lone parents who are students can claim Housing Benefit. If you own your own home you will not receive Housing Benefit to help pay a mortgage but you can get extra Income Support to pay the mortgage interest.

If you are eligible for Income Support and need to claim Housing Benefit, you will have to go first to the Benefit Agency to put in your claims. When you claim Income Support you will be asked to fill in a Housing Benefit Application Form which is then forwarded on to your local Council by the Benefit Agency. Housing Association or private tenants will be sent another form to complete by the council giving details of how much rent they pay. Lone parents who are not on Income Support but who want to claim Housing Benefit must go directly to the Council's Housing Benefit and Council Tax Departments.

Lone parents on Income Support can get all their rent paid, but if your income is above Income Support level any help with rent is reduced 65 pence for each £1.00 above the Income Support Level.

You can also make a back-claim for up to 52 weeks but only if you can show you had 'good cause' for not making the claim before. This might be because you were wrongly advised or were ill. Housing Benefit will only be paid to cover rent on property charges, so if your rent bill contains an amount for heating or other services this will not be covered. If you have any non-dependents living with you they will be expected to contribute to housing costs so your benefit will be reduced. It may also be reduced if you are judged to be paying an unreasonably high rent. If your circumstances change you have to inform the Housing Benefit Department because any 'overpayment' can be reclaimed.

You should receive a full breakdown of your Housing Benefit. If you disagree with any part of your assessment you can ask for the decision to be reviewed, and if you remain unsatisfied you can go to a Review Board and be represented there.

The Council Tax and reducing payments

The Council Tax works on the basis of one bill for each dwelling. The Bill itself contains a Property Element (50%) and a Personal Element (50%). Properties are banded from A (under £40,000) to H (over £320,000). The Charge for Band D is a norm of 100% against which the other bands will be charged as a proportion. So Band A bills are 67% of Band D, and Band H are 200% of Band D.

The liability to pay the Council Tax Bill can be shared between a number of residents, depending upon their ranking in a hierarchy of residents. This means that where there is a freeholder, leaseholder, secure tenant, licensee and so on the liability falls on those who share the highest ranking in the hierarchy. So where the freeholder lives in the property he or she has to pay but the tenant does not.

There are four ways in which the individual's bill can be reduced. These include a Disability Reduction Scheme, a Discount, a Transitional Reduction Scheme, and either Council Tax Benefit or 'Second Adult Rebate', whichever is higher.

The Disability Reduction Scheme covers situations where one or more people, including children, are disabled and the property has to have special features to provide for their needs. In these circumstances the Council Tax Bill is reduced to the Band immediately below the Band at which the property was originally estimated, except where the property is already in Band A.

Discounts are given on the Council Tax Bill against

the Personal Element where there is only one 'visible' adult living in the house who does not have a 'status discount', or where the property is empty. The 'visible' adult status applies to any liable adult living in the dwelling. This status contrasts with that of the 'invisible' adult who is discounted. Invisible adults are adults living in the dwelling who for special reasons are not counted as liable for the bill. These include –

- *anyone under 19 for whom Child Benefit is paid*
- *school leavers under 20 (who if they left school after April 30th get discount status until 1st November)*
- *Registered students*
- *Hospital patients*
- *Prisoners*
- *People who are severely mentally impaired*
- *Apprentices and trainees on Youth Training*

Where these circumstances apply, the Visible Adult gets a reduction of 25% of the Personal Element of the Council Tax Bill.

Transitional reduction aims to limit the increase in the changeover from Community Charge to the Council Tax. It is awarded automatically by the Local Authority to any qualifying dwelling to any eligible person. You are eligible if you live in a qualifying dwelling and it was your sole or main residence on 31st March 1993. This is a complicated scheme so you may wish to seek further advice on how the sum has been worked out.

Finally, there are two types of Council Tax Benefit. The first is known as *Main Council Tax Benefit*, the second *Alternative Maximum Council Tax Benefit* *(more commonly known as Second Adult Rebate)*.

To be eligible for Main CTB you must be resident in

the dwelling, liable to pay the Council Tax bill and have less than £16,000 capital. This rule about capital does not apply to Second Adult Rebate. Where a liable person satisfies the conditions for both types of CTB, he or she will be awarded the type that gives them the highest amount of entitlement. If you are on Income Support you must claim CTB from the Benefits Agency. Anyone else must go to the Local Authority Housing Benefit and Council Tax Benefit Office to make a claim.

To work out your entitlement you must first work out the nett liability for Council Tax by deducting any sum for disability reduction, discount or transitional reduction. This gives you the applicable amount. You then calculate your income as you do for Income Support. If your income is lower or the same as the applicable amount, you receive the Maximum CTB. If it is higher, you reduce the maximum CTB by 20% of the excess income.

Child Benefit and One Parent Benefit

Child Benefit is a tax-free, cash payment for families with children paid to the parent who is responsible for the children, from the Monday following the birth of a child. In addition, lone parents get One Parent Benefit. This can be paid to others bringing up a child alone, such as a grandparent, but not to widows who receive Widowed Mother's Allowance.

Lone parents can ask for child benefit to be paid weekly – most other families get it every four weeks – and it can be paid through an order book cashed at the Post Office or directly into your bank. These benefits are normally paid until the child is 16, but up to 19 if the child is in full time education, but not if they are in work or on a youth training programme.

The rate of these benefits are:

Child Benefit - for first or eldest child £10.00
Child Benefit - for each further child £ 8.10
One Parent Benefit £ 6.05

Both these benefits count as income when Income Support is being calculated, so it will be reduced by the amount of Child Benefit and One Parent Benefit received. They are also counted as income in the calculation of Housing Benefit and Council Tax Benefit, but they do not count at all in the calculation of Family Credit.

Anyone claiming Widow's Benefit or any other long term benefit such as Retirement Pension should claim Child Benefit because they will be worse off unless they do, but they cannot claim one parent benefit because these benefits already have an additional amount that can be claimed for dependents.

Unemployment Benefit

Unemployment benefit is paid fortnightly in arrears and is taxable. In order to claim Unemployment Benefit you have to have paid class one National Insurance contributions for periods of time, be unemployed but available for work and prove that you are actively seeking work. You also have to sign on, usually about once a fortnight at your local Unemployment Benefit Office. Not many lone parents claim Unemployment Benefit because they are not required to sign on, and often have few National Insurance Contributions. In addition they are not likely to be better off on Unemployment Benefit because they are likely to be eligible for an Income Support top-up. However, some lone parents who get a reasonable amount of child maintenance or have savings between £3,000-8,000.00 might be better off claiming Unemployment Benefit, especially as Child and One Parent Benefits are paid on top. If you want to return to work in the near future, signing on as available for work not only means you will count in the statistics of the unemployed, it also means you get good access to other employment services that can help you, although these are increasingly being made available to lone parents who do not sign on.

Tax

The tax year runs from 6th April in one year to 5th April in the next, although there are proposals for this to change. How much tax you owe is assessed on all the income you receive in this period, minus certain amounts which are known as allowances and are tax free.

Lone parents are entitled to two allowances, the Single Person's Allowance and Additional Personal Allowance, which together add up to the same amount as a Married Couple's Allowance. You get the Additional Personal Allowance if your child lives with you for all or part of the tax year, until the child leaves full-time education, even where the child's father pays maintenance and he claims the Married Couple's Allowance. If the child stays with you and the father for respective portions of the tax year the Additional Personal Allowance might be split between you.

Tax on any maintenance paid is complicated

because the system changed in 1989, so effectively two systems are in operation. Deduction of tax from maintenance was abolished from April 6th 1989. Payments made under the old system attract tax relief for the ex-husband or wife who pays and are taxable on the income of the ex-husband or wife who receives the maintenance. If you reach a maintenance agreement, or have an order now and are the payer, you can claim up to £1,720 per year tax relief on any spousal or child maintenance paid. If the payee remarries, the tax relief stops. Unmarried parents cannot claim tax relief, but the recipient is not liable for any tax on maintenance received. For Court orders applied for before 15th March 1988 and sent to Inland Revenue before 30th June 1988, the payer receives full tax relief on any amount paid, but the payee must pay tax on any amount received. If that amount increased any time after 5th April 1989, the amount of tax the payee must pay is pegged forever to the amount taxable in the 1988-89 year.

Widows are entitled to the Widow's Bereavement Allowance of £1,720 for the year in which the husband dies providing they have lived with him for part of the tax year. They can also claim any portion of the married couple's allowance not used up by the husbaand before death. They can claim bereavement allowance again in the next year providing they have not remarried before the start of the tax year. If in these two years they have a child they will receive £3,445 plus £1,720, plus £1,720.

In subsequent years widows receive just the personal and additional personal allowances. They are also likely to pay more income tax than other lone parents as their widowed Mother's Allowance or Widow's Pension of £56.10 per week is taxed. But the Child Dependency Addition on Widowed Mother's Allowance of £10.95 is not taxed.

The forms of tax relief you should investigate include any relief on mortgage interest which is payable for interest up to £30,000 – this may be available at source (MIRAS) – and tax payable on interest from banks and building societies. Depositors have deductions of 5% made at source, but depositors who are not liable for tax can complete a registration form (R85) and interest will be paid gross.

National Insurance Contributions

These payments form the basis for National Insurance Benefits and are paid at £1.12 on earnings over £56 per week and 9% on the rest of your earnings up to a ceiling of £420 per week. Any earnings over this amount for employed persons are not subject to NI contributions.

CHILD MAINTENANCE AND THE CHILD SUPPORT AGENCY

Introduction

As long as 20 years ago government committees were recommending that something serious should be done about the failure of ex-partners to pay maintenance for children. Yet as short a time ago as 1992 only about 3 out of 10 lone parents received any regular child maintenance. The amounts paid were very low and, as all orders for maintenance, including any increases, had to be taken through the courts, the whole process was cumbersome. For unmarried mothers in particular, trying to get a court order for maintenance could be harrowing.

What the Child Support Agency will do

In 1991 a new Act of Parliament was passed setting up a new agency – The Child Support Agency – a new section of the DSS whose job is to track down the missing partner, assess their contribution for maintenance and get them to pay. When it is fully operational in April 1997 the Agency will take over most of the functions in deciding maintenance that the courts have carried out. The courts will still deal with disputes about paternity; maintenance claims for the ex-spouse where the partners have been married, or where the ex-partner does not live in the UK; for extra costs for disabled children; where ex-partners have considerable income and you want to claim for more than you would get through the Agency's assessment. If you have an existing court order it will continue to be dealt with by the courts until the Child Support Agency is fully operational.

Child Support Agency terminology

The Agency employs a new language to describe its customers and their relationship to the child. The terms used by the Agency have caused offence in some quarters. They call the non-residential parent the *'absent parent'*. The parent with whom the children are living is called the *'parent with care'*. Some parents, particularly the *'absent parent'* with a close relationship with their children, object because it makes it sound as if they have run away from their children and no longer care for them. But as these are the terms set out within the law, we will all have to get used to using them.

The formula for calculating maintenance payments

The Agency operates a somewhat complicated formula based upon social security rates to assess the level of liability, and take into account the earnings and reasonable expenses of both the parents. It is expected that this formula will put up considerably the amounts paid in maintenance. You will need some expert advice about how to work out the formula. This you can get from the Agency itself, but there are fees to be paid for anyone not on benefits. The Agency also has the power to seek a deduction of earnings order from the absent parent. The basis of the formula is that the Income Support Rates for the Parent with Care and each child are added up. This gives the Maintenance Requirement amount. Next the absent parent's income after tax and National Insurance deductions has to be assessed. The Absent Parent takes out the amounts for reasonable housing costs, and the Income Support rates for their Personal Allowance and any natural children living with them, ie children by birth or adoption for whom they are financially responsible. Once this deduction has been made you are left with the 'Assessable Income'. Half of the assessable income then goes towards paying the Maintenance Requirement. If there is any Assessable Income left over once the Maintenance Requirement has been paid, that further sum can be assessed for maintenance at a rate of 25%.

How the Services will work and who can use them

The Child Support Agency is phasing in its dealing with cases, but the Agency's services are open to deal with all new maintenance claims whether the applicant is in work or on benefits. Either parent can use the CAS for a maintenance assessment and to collect and enforce all maintenance payments. There is a fee payable for all services for those not on Income Support, Family Credit or Disability Working Allowance. All lone parents in receipt of these benefits will be obliged to get a maintenance assessment but will not pay a fee. Lone parents in work can choose to use the Agency's services.

LONE PARENT SURVIVAL GUIDE

If you are using the Agency you will fill in and return a Child Support Maintenance Application form. The CSA uses the information you give to track down the absent parent and then sends them a Maintenance Enquiry form. This is filled in and returned. The CSA makes the calculation and notifies both parents. Payment should then start.

Lone parents on benefit and the requirement to cooperate

All lone parents on benefit will be asked to give information about their ex-partner so that the Agency can follow them up, assess their maintenance liability and get them to pay. Lone parents are now required to cooperate with the Agency, but there will be a number of lone parents who do not want to give the Agency the information they require. In these cases the Agency will want to know whether or not the parent has *'good cause'* for refusing the information. The idea of *'good cause'* is any reason that the parent with care has for thinking that disclosing the information will bring undue harm or distress to themselves or the children.

In these cases the lone parent will be called to an interview and should receive a leaflet telling them about what will happen in the interview and future procedure entitled *Your Rights at the Interview*. They do not have to produce proof of their reasons, providing the story is internally consistent it will be believed. The Child Support Officer will judge whether or not the reasons are sufficient to waive the condition of the parent's cooperation. If they think it is sufficient nothing further will happen. If they do not accept the reasons, there will be an explanation and written reasons for non-acceptance and further interviews. But the parent with care could end having her or his benefit reduced for up to 18 months. Even in this situation the Child Support Officer who reviews the case has to take into account the welfare of the child before deduction is made. If they decide to reduce the benefit the parent with care can appeal to a tribunal.

It is difficult to tell what reasons will be accepted as sufficient reason but there are a lot of circumstances to take into account and a lot of this ground will be established as cases are dealt with. It would be wise to take a friend or an adviser with you to the interview and to take notes of the proceedings. In any case, if you get called to interview you should seek advice from your local Citizen's Advice Bureau or other advice agency.

Advantages and disadvantages of the new system

There are a number of advantages in the new system. More lone parents will get child maintenance, and lone parents in work and on Family Credit get to keep £15.00 of the amount before their income is assessed for Family Credit. In addition the sum will be reviewed annually and the amonts used to calculate the formula will be raised annually in line with inflation. There are problems for these lone parents because their Family Credit is only assessed every 26 weeks and cannot be varied, so if the maintenance dries up during this period they could face hardship.

Unfortunately lone parents on Income Support will be no better off and may well end up more financially insecure as they will now rely upon several different sources of income. However, any lone parent on Income Support who does not receive the maintenance they should be getting can get their benefit topped up by the Benefits Agency to meet the gap. Those lone parents who get enough in maintenance to mean that they are no longer entitled to receive Income Support will also lose the string of other benefits such as free school meals and health benefits that you can claim if you receive Income Support.

The Child Support Agency represents a massive change in one parent family life and many different agencies are monitoring its progress and problems in order as far as possible to put the problems right. If you do have a problem go to a local advice agency, because as well as helping you, they will want to monitor what happens to you for the benefit of others.

HOUSING AND HOMELESSNESS – KEEPING A ROOF OVER YOUR HEADS

When a relationship ends there is a strong urge to move out as quickly as possible in order to make a new start and to escape from the emotional stress. But if you want to keep a roof over your heads, this could be a bad move. Only move out if you have somewhere permanent to go and are sure that you do not have the legal right to stay in the home.

Lone parents living in Council or Housing Association properties

About 6 out of 10 lone parents live in council accommodation. Many have sought help from the council under the procedures covering homelessness.

The right to stay in the home depends upon whether or not you are married to your partner and what sort of tenancy you have. If you have been widowed and the tenancy was a joint one you become the sole tenant, but even where the tenancy was not in your name, it may be possible that it will pass to you as most councils allow the tenancy to pass on to a close relative. If you are married it does not matter whose name is on the tenancy, you have the right to stay unless a court orders you to leave. You will lose this right when you are divorced unless a court extends it. If you are not married you have the right to stay if the tenancy is in your name or in both your names, but not if the tenancy is in your partner's name alone.

In certain circumstances you can have the tenancy transferred into your name. This can happen through the court where you are married but taking divorce or judicial separation proceedings. It can take a long time, particularly if you are in dispute about other issues in the divorce. The court has less power to transfer tenancies in the case of unmarried partners, although it can do so in some cases. You should seek legal advice about this, but your main course of action is to talk to the council or housing association who may be able to offer a new tenancy elsewhere. Whatever your marital circumstances, if the tenancy is a joint one you may end up having to pay all the rent if your partner stops paying. If you get into trouble on this issue you should contact your council or housing association immediately. If you are married but the tenancy is in your partner's name, the renting authority can accept rent from you even if your partner has left, although they may not wish to do so if you do not have a long-term, legal right to stay.

If you do have a secure tenancy there are a range of things you can do with your home. The tenancy can be passed on once to a close relative who has been living with you for at least 12 months, but if your partner has passed it on to you this counts as the 'once'. You can take in lodgers without asking permission and may sublet if you get written consent, but if you sublet the whole of your home you lose security of tenure and the council or housing association can get an order to evict you. You may also have the right to buy your home on a mortgage or on part-buy and part-rent under the Shared Ownership Scheme.

It is the responsibility of the council or housing association to repair the structure and exterior the property. If you have trouble getting repairs done you may be able to pay for it yourself and reclaim it under The Housing and Building Control Act 1984. But get advice first.

If you do want to move you can try for a council transfer, but probably need to show good reason as to why you need to move such as ill health, or needing to be near your family. Getting support from a social worker, health visitor or doctor can help. You can also exchange your property with another council tenant. You need your landlord's permission to do this and can get information about the Tenant's Exchange Scheme through the council's housing office, or by telephoning the Housing Organisations Mobility and Exchange Services on 071 222 0357.

If your partner has been violent, you can get a court order called an injunction to prevent them molesting you or the children, and in serious cases you can get them removed from the home by obtaining an exclusion order, which lasts for three months but can be renewed. If you do have a legal right to stay but have already left home with the children the courts can make an order enabling you to return home. If you left because of threats or episodes of violence and are too scared to return, you will be considered homeless, and if in 'priority need'.

See later sections – *What to do if you are facing homelessness* and *What the law defines* – you will get help from the council.

Lone parents who are home owners

Experience indicates that when a relationship breaks down, bills go unpaid. In the case of a mortgage this can end up with serious consequences such as home repossession. You must first check that the mortgage payments are still being made and ensure that you are claiming all the money you can. Most building societies and other lenders are used to dealing with these circumstances and will try to be helpful, providing you do not delay in informing them of the position and discussing solutions. If you have the right to stay in the property, you must discuss with the mortgage lender methods for payment so that arrears do not build up. They may agree to lengthen the period of years for which the mortgage has been taken to make the regular payments less. They may accept an interest-only payment. You can get Mortgage Tax Relief on up to £30,000.00, and if you are receiving Income Support you will have your mortgage interest paid for you. But first you must find out if you have the right to stay in the property.

If your partner has died and the property was held in joint names it will normally pass to you whether you were married or not, unless your partner's share forms part of their estate. If the property was in your partner's name its future will be determined either by the will or by the rules of Intestacy. By these rules a surviving spouse will benefit, but not someone who was not married to the deceased. A divorced spouse and anyone being maintained by the deceased may have a claim against the estate. If you put money into the house you may have a claim to a share of it, but if you have no right to it you will have to leave when it is sold. You should not leave until forced to do so, because this will affect your right to council help with housing.

If your partner left you, your rights depend upon

your marital status, your financial contribution to the house and who is named as home owner. If you are married you have the right to stay unless a court orders you to leave. You lose this right on divorce unless a court extends it. If the home is owned solely by you or jointly, it cannot be sold without your agreement. If it is your partner's name alone you can protect your rights by registering a charge on the property under the Matrimonial Homes Act 1983 which stops your partner selling without your knowledge

If you are unmarried you can clearly stay if you are sole or joint owner, but if it is in your partner's name alone you may not have the right to stay and may have to leave after reasonable notice. You may have acquired a legal share in the house through making financial contributions or if you had an agreement registering this when you moved in. If you are solely or jointly own the property it cannot be sold without your agreement, but if it is in your partner's name alone, you may not be able to prevent its sale. If you have faced problems of violence from your partner you have the same rights to get court injunctions and exclusion orders that were described for those renting accommodation.

The courts can order the transfer of property when relationships break down whether you are married or not, but they will only do so rarely for the benefit of children under the Children Act 1989 for unmarried couples. Nevertheless, they can determine your relative shares in the property or postpone a sale until chidren are grown up. Where married partners are divorcing, the courts have wide powers to transfer the home or a share of it, to order a sale

and divide the proceeds between you, or to postpone a sale in the interests of the children.
If you receive Legal Aid to sort out your problems with the home in the courts, a *'charge'* can be made against the future sale of the property to recover these costs.
In the past, a rough rule of thumb has been for the parent with the children to get the house as a kind of compenstion for the loss of pension rights. This has been the case where women have not worked and do not get pension rights for themselves. The house became an accumulating asset to offset against their old age. Often there was a deal which involved

small amounts of cash maintenance for children, plus the house. It is not yet clearly understood what impact the Child Support Act will have on the courts' decisions on property. As reasonable housing costs are taken into account in the calculation, the government thinks there will not be any change, but some legal commentators think that the tendency will be for solicitors to advise their clients not to agree to transfers of property because they can both get an equity in the house and their future housing costs offset against child maintenance payments.

Lone parents in private rented accommodation

Where you have a protected or assured tenancy, the rules for deciding whether or not you have the right to remain in private rented accommodation, or what to do about violence and transfers of tenancy, are very similar to those for council accommodation. In most cases you cannot be forced to leave without a court order. The first thing to check is the nature of the tenancy agreement between you and the landlord.

This is a complicated area of the law as there are several types and you should seek advice. The nature of the tenancy governs things like whether you can pass on a tenancy to your children, get your rent reduced, or force your landlord to do repairs. To fully work out your options you should also check the policy of your local council, because the guidelines from the Department of the Environment strongly encourage councils not to force tenants to stay where the outcome of a court case would clearly lead to an eviction. But if you need to get help from the council you must not have made yourself *'intentionally homeless'* – and they may not follow the guidelines – so check the local rules.

If the landlord wants to evict you he must first give you written *'notice to quit'* or *'notice to seek possession'* before applying to the court and you should immediately seek advice. The landlord has to prove either that he now needs the house for personal occupation, or that you have broken one of a number of rules which include not having paid your rent for a period, having caused damage to the property, or having caused a nuisance to the neighbours.

If you have the kind of landlord who attempts to harass you out of the property without taking the necessary legal steps, go to the council who should have a tenancy relations officer who can take action on your behalf, including court action against your landlord.

What to do if you are facing homelessness

If you are facing homelessness, the first thing to do is to try to prevent it by getting all the money and legal help you can to stay in the home. But if it cannot be prevented the local council have a legal duty to help you. If you have nowhere to sleep that night you should contact the housing department who should arrange overnight accommodation. If the problem arises after office hours there should be an emergency worker on duty and you can either phone the town hall or the police station to find out how to contact them.

After dealing with the immediate problem you will be asked for detailed information to make sure that you are homeless or threatened with homelessness, in *'priority need'* and have not made yourself intentionally homeless. If they accept this they must either help you to stay in your own home or find alternative accommodation which may be in another local authority area if you have a local connection there.

While they investigate your case they must provide you with temporary accommodation such as a hostel or bed and breakfast accommodation. Even after you have been accepted for permanent rehousing you may have to spend some time in bed and breakfast accommodation before you are given an offer of a property.

What the law defines as homelessness and in priority need

You are homeless if you have nowhere where you and the children can live together, where you cannot get into your home or have been forced to leave because of violence. If you have to leave within 28 days you are threatened with homelessness. The Council may insist that you get evicted before they help you, although they should not do this if you are living with family or friends. They may also want proof of violence such as an injunction, but they should provide temporary accommodation while they investigate. They may also want you to get an exclusion order forcing the violent partner to leave, but the courts will only do this if you want to go back and live in the home and it is safe for you to do so. You are in priority need if you have dependent children or are pregnant, vulnerable because of age or mental or physical illness or disability or have lost your home through fire, flood or other disaster. You do not have to have the children live with you all the time to qualify. They can split their time with another parent or carer. If the children normally live with you, or would if you had a home, you are still in priority need because the law accepts that families should not be split up as a result of homelessness. This rule applies if it is suggested that the children might go into care. The council should house you all together, and if any attempt is made to take children into care you should immediately contact a help agency.

Intentional homelessness
If the housing department decide that it is your own fault that you are homeless because you deliberately did not pay the rent, for example, they do not have a duty to re-house you, but still have to give advice as to where to find accommodation. You must explain all your circumstances to the housing department because you may have got into financial difficulties through no fault of your own such as losing your job. The housing department should give their reasons for not helping you in writing and if you disagree with their decision go to a local advice centre.

If the council has a duty to help you they must also arrange for your belongings to be stored although they may want to charge you for this. If you receive Income Support you can argue that this is unreasonable.

One offer policies
Increasingly, because of the shortage of housing,

ESSENTIAL

local councils only make one offer of accommodation and, if you refuse, they may not offer any further help. The offer may be in council, housing association or private accommodation. The council has to ensure it is long-term and settled accommodation. You should take advice before turning down an offer.

GETTING BACK TO WORK

Why work?

At present, the majority of lone parents are living on Income Support, but a recent government survey showed that 95% want to go back to work at some time. There may be many reasons why you want to get paid work, and these could include –

- *getting to meet people* – being a lone parent can sometimes be very lonely.
- *using your past experience* – you may feel that you will get rusty if you do not get the opportunity to use skills and knowledge you have used in the past.
- *increasing your self-confidence* – if you have been at home alone with just your children you may feel insecure in situations where you had previously coped with no difficulty.
- *following a career* – your career may have been interrupted by having children or the breakdown of a relationship.
- *status* – for many people having a job makes them feel more accepted.
- *self-respect/self-fulfilment* – it may be important to how you feel about yourself.
- *planning for the future* – you may have long-term aims or wish to make sure that you will be financially secure when your children have left home.
- *something to offer* – you may feel that you want to contribute something to society, or to help a particular group in your chosen field.
- *need to earn money* – Money is important, but as you can see there are other reasons which may influence your wish to return to work.

ESSENTIAL

Problems to be overcome

If you do decide that you want to work, either full or part time, you need to think about how it will affect your income, because there are expenses to be met if you work.

Childcare costs are likely to be your most expensive item but you will also have to take into account how much it costs to get to work, whether or not you need to buy new or different clothes and the costs of other work expenses such as lunches. On the other hand if you are out at work all day you are probably saving money on heating, and you may have things like a subsidised canteen.

Some lone parents worry about the demands of managing a home and a job without a lot of support. It can be difficult to balance the demands of work and children in any circumstances. It is much harder if you are doing it alone. But being at home can be isolating and lonely. Working and learning to see yourself as a competent and skilful person can give you a more positive outlook on life, and you may have lots of energy because you are enjoying yourself in your job.

Benefits and work

If you work less than 16 hours you will probably be claiming Income Support and can earn £15.00 per week before you lose benefit pound for pound. If you are intending to work 16 hours or more a week and you are on benefits you will need to plan carefully. You will need to look at what your situation is at the moment and match this against how much you would need to earn for you to be better off going out to work.

LONE PARENT SURVIVAL GUIDE

For many lone parents this can be a daunting calculation, but you can get help.
The Benefits Agency and Citizens' Advice Bureaux have people who can help you make the calculation about whether or not you would be better off if you took a job. Many also have access to computer programmes that make the arithmetic easier.

How to calculate income

You need to calculate your weekly income, noting how much income you receive from –

- **means tested benefits** – *Income Support, Family Credit, Council Tax Benefit, Housing Benefit, Disability Working Allowance.*
- **other benefits** – *which are paid regardless of what you earn. The most important of these are Child Benefit and One Parent Benefit.*
- **maintenance** – *either for you or for your children.*

If you work over 16 hours you may be entitled to Family Credit. What you receive will depend on the amount you earn and the number and ages of your children. If you receive maintenance, £15.00 of this will be ignored when calculating your entitlement. The table below shows the differences in what you get on Income Support and Family Credit.

Income Support	*Family Credit*
You *will* receive	**You *will* receive**
Housing Benefit	*Free prescriptions*
Mortgage interest	*Free optical treatment*
Council Tax Benefit	*Free dental treatment*
Free prescriptions	
Free optical treatment	**You *may* receive**
Free dental treatment	*Housing Benefit*
Free school meals	*Council Tax Benefit*

When you work you will also receive *Child Benefit* and *One Parent Benefit*.

As you can see, working out if you will be better off may take you some time.

Making the change from benefits to work

There is likely to be a short period as you start work and come off benefits when you are not receiving any money. This can be difficult as you will still be expected to meet your usual weekly outgoings. But if you are transferring from Income Support to Family Credit and you have just started a new job, you can ask for your claim to be processed by the *fast tracking* system. This means your claim should be completed in about six days instead of the more usual three to four weeks.

LONE PARENT SURVIVAL GUIDE

There are other possible options to get you through this difficult phase. You could ask your employer for an advance on your pay. You may be able to get a Crisis Loan from the Social Fund, and it might be worth thinking about a bank loan – although this would mean having to pay interest on it, so you should think about it carefully.

Because the position of lone parents is so vulnerable, you clearly need to check carefully that you will be better off in work. For many lone parents the costs of childcare and other work expenses mean that they will not be better off and may be a lot worse off, depending upon what they can earn. Your wish to work may be strong enough to sustain small losses in income, but you may need to re-think the project if the losses are too great and wait for a time when the expenses of things like childcare get cheaper – such as when your youngest child is at school. The following check list will help you to calculate your own situation.

Check list on financial situation

Income	If I took a job	At the moment
Earnings		
Child benefit		
One Parent benefit		
Maintenance		
Income support or		
Family credit		
Housing benefit		
Council tax benefit		
Other income/benefit		
TOTAL INCOME		

Expenses	If I took a job	At the moment
Rent/mortgage		
Food		
Council tax		
Electricity		
Childcare cost		
Travel		
Clothes/equipment for work		
School meals		
Newspapers/cigarettes etc		
Entertainment		
Any other expenses		

TOTAL EXPENSES

What to do about childcare

There is no doubt that childcare is the biggest single barrier to lone parents being able to work. If you have to pay the full cost of daycare it can be very expensive, particularly on a small wage. It can also be difficult to find the kind of childcare that gives you the peace of mind you need in knowing that your child is being well looked after while you work.

Childminders

Childminders are a very big source of childcare support for working parents. They vary enormously in what they offer, the level of training they have received and how well they look after children. Good childminders who are flexible and work with you are worth their weight in gold. To find one you can get a list from you local council social services department who, under the 1989 Children Act have to *'register'* them. Indeed all who care for children under 8 now have to be registered. This means that they will have been checked for criminal records and that the house has been inspected on its safety and suitability for young children.

Whilst you get the name and address of the minder from your council, you have to come to an agreement with her on what you will pay, for how many hours care, arrangements about family holidays and so on. It is vital that you reach a clear, written agreement with the childminder so that you both know what to expect. The Council may well issue draft contracts to its childminders.

There is nothing quite like the worry of a parent about how their vulnerable child is faring in someone else's care. So when you have to choose a childminder there are a number of factors to bear in mind including –

- *Is the childminder registered with the Social Services Department?*
- *Do you feel comfortable when you walk into the house?*
- *How many other children are there and what are their ages?*
- *What kind of food are the children given?*
- *What kind of toys are available?*
- *Where, when and for how long do the children sleep?*
- *Does the childminder smoke?*
- *Do you and the childminder share the same views on discipline and behaviour?*

Remember that you have to work at the relationship with your childminder. Sometimes if you get on well with the person you can forget that they are earning their living through childminding. You must always remind yourself that in a far less formal way you are in fact in the same position to them that your employer is to you – you must not abuse their goodwill and friendship, or resentments will build up.

Nurseries

You may want your child to go to a full time nursery. Whether these are run by the local authority or privately, they will be registered. You should check on elements like the space and facilities *(including outdoor playspace)*, opening times and dates, qualifications and experience of staff – and rate of staff turnover – and the level of parental involvement. The level of fees and any likely increases will be vital factors for you. Some local councils do have low cost or free nursery places, but these mostly go to children in extreme need.

Other options

There are other options in childcare. Playgroups serve a very useful function for the younger child and they can be invaluable for children in one parent families who may be isolated from other children and need structured play experiences. They are not often convenient for working parents, but if you use a childminder you may well find that she will take your child to a playgroup. Some local councils run nursery classes attached to infant schools. These normally offer half day sessions and will probably have waiting lists. They are wonderful educational opportunities for children, but again they are not geared to cater for working parents. If you get a place for your child you will need a childminder who can take or pick up or both depending on your working pattern. Sometimes other mothers with children at the school also do childminding. It is also worth asking the teacher if she knows of anyone, or investigating via the parents' group.

Some employers offer workplace nurseries at a subsidised rate for their staff. Others may offer vouchers to help you pay the costs. These work benefits are few and far between at present, but a number of companies are thinking about introducing them.

School age children

As childcare for the younger child can be expensive, lone parents often plan to start work when their youngest child has reached school age and the costs of care go down considerably. There are a range of after school and holiday clubs for school age children. These may run in your child's school or pick children up from nearby schools, but they are designed to provide a range of stimulating activities for children and to meet the needs of working parents. As with other forms of care, you can get details from the local council.

Identifying your skills

If you are a lone parent you may be very isolated and this can undermine your confidence. It is easy to think that it will be difficult to find work and that you have nothing to offer. Anyone who hasn't worked for some time suffers from a lack of confidence, but you have to recognise the things you can do in order to present yourself in a positive way.

You may never have had a job or you could have been away from work for some time. Whichever is the case it is important that you identify your abilities and knowledge and see them as useful tools which will help you re-enter employment.

As a lone parent you have a considerable range of skills. You are –

- *extremely resourceful*
- *good at managing money*
- *excellent at negotiating with officials*
- *able to prioritise conflicting demands on your time*
- *quick decision-maker*

Transferable skills

Many of the skills you use daily are transferable to a work situation, communication skills are an obvious example. You are likely to spend a great deal of time each day talking to people, making sure they understand what you want, getting them to do something for you and giving or receiving information. Sometimes you will need to put this in writing, often keeping a record and putting it somewhere safe for future reference.

How do you identify the skills you possess that could be useful?

First look at the following definitions:

Skill – an ability to do something

Examples: drive a car, write reports, wordprocess, keep accounts, counsel, file, time-keep, use the telephone.

Experience – regular or frequent use of a skill

Examples: work as a mini-cab driver, use a switchboard, organise events, maintain a filing system

Knowledge – facts/information you have acquired

Examples: historic facts/dates, knowing how to mend electrical appliances, academic qualifications.

For example, you learn a wordprocessing package (knowledge), you get a job where you spend 50% of your time using it (experience) and can write and edit reports at 45 words a minute (skill).

Now write down all your experiences of paid and unpaid employment and voluntary activities.

Note down the skills and knowledge you use, or have used, for each area of experience. You will find you finish up with a long list.

Your list of experiences probably included activities

for which you received no payment. It is important to look at these carefully as they often provide evidence that you are able to do a job.

Once you have worked out what your skills are and what you have to offer you will need to match this to jobs you want to apply for.

If you find there is a large gap between what you would like to do and what you think someone might employ you to do then think again and ask yourself these questions –

- *Are you underselling yourself – have you given yourself proper credit for the skills you have?*
- *Have you got some, but not all, of the experience/skills asked for? It may still be worthwhile having a try. You may be better than the other candidates or they may be willing to provide training.*
- *Do you need to build in extra steps eg some training or voluntary work to increase you skills.*

Planning for the future

Lone parents have to plan for the future. It may be impossible to take a job now because you cannot earn enough, or you may have been through a messy separation with your partner and need time to recover from the hurt and upset. There may be more practical reasons for not being able to work. You may have very rusty work skills and need some specific training to help get you a decent job. There is always a tendency to put off thinking about getting back into work but, if you mean business, you have to have a practical plan that can be put into practice bit by bit to get you nearer your goal.

How to plan –

- *What kind of work do you want to do?*
- *What kind of training or other activity do need to undertake to achieve your goals?*
- *What sort of people or agencies do you need to help you?*
- *What stages do you need to take to get you to your goal?*
- *How long should each action take?*
- *What kind of problems do you face and what can you practically do about them?*

You need to review your plan at intervals to see how it is working out, and you may need to revise it in light of experience.

You can get help to write up your plan. It might help to see a Careers Adviser from your local Training and Enterprise Council *(TEC)* or local council Careers Service. There may be a local education advice centre. Local college and other providers offer training for work skills. As a lone parent you may get some help in paying for childcare while you train from your local TEC.

If you are ready for work you might want to go to a Job Club which can help you in the search for a job. You can also get help in Job Clubs to write your CV and fill out application forms for jobs.

LEISURE AND HOLIDAYS

Introduction

Many lone parents experience stress, loneliness, and overwhelming responsibilities, especially those struggling to cope on a low income. If you are in these circumstances, planning some leisure time for yourself or taking a holiday can make all the difference.

Most lone parents report that it is very difficult for them to get any time for themselves. But you will need some time apart from the children to keep your own identity intact, to keep a sense of proportion about the difficulties you face and to have some fun doing the things that you like rather than meeting only your children's needs, however much fun this may often be. Hopefully you will have the kind of friends who will occasionally babysit for you to let you go out.

There are also a range of self help groups for lone parents who organise outings for parents and children. They also run babysitting and other very useful services. The best known of these groups is Gingerbread and their national office can let you have details of their local groups. If no local Gingerbread Group exists there may well be others near you that are not part of the Gingerbread Network. The National Council for One Parent Families has a national database of lone parents groups, or you could find out about them from the local library.

The occasional holiday can work wonders. Holidays play an increasing part in people's expectations, yet surveys have shown that 40% of people in Britain take no holiday in any given year. The great majority

LONE PARENT SURVIVAL GUIDE

give as their reason that they cannot afford one, or that they prefer *(or need)* to spend the money on something else.

As a lone parent you may have to cut the cost of a holiday to rock bottom, but there are a number of options open to you to get a holiday and they are all worth pursuing.

There are one or two general things you should know –

- *Parents are legally entitled to take children out of school for two weeks for the purpose of a family holiday. Out of season prices are much lower than the main holiday period (July/August) so, for younger children not yet caught up with exams, May, early June and September/October can be cheaper and far less crowded.*
- *Bargains can also be found at short notice, when unsold holiday packages are discounted.*
- *For self-catering holidays, a larger unit shared between two or more families can work out cheaper, and be more fun.*
- *Group bookings, both for accommodation (particularly out of season) and for 'attractions', are often charged at reduced rates. It is always worth enquiring when you make a booking.*
- *For group travel, hiring a minibus may work out cheaper than using public transport.*
- *A Savings Scheme, to spread the cost of the holiday over a period of time, is operated by SPLASH, the company specialising in One Parent Family travel (see address list).*
- *Remember that good value holidays go quickly, so book as early as possible unless you are taking a chance on a last-minute bargain.*

Many of the organisations listed are charities operating on a small budget – when writing for information, please enclose a stamped addressed envelope.

Local councils can sometimes help with finance for holidays in special circumstances: in cases of handicap or illness, for example, but not when low income is the only reason for a family being unable to take a holiday. It may also be possible to arrange for respite care for a person suffering from a severe disability, so that the rest of the family can have a holiday.

Trusts, as well as support groups, exist to help people suffering from a particular disability or disease. Some have specially designed holiday centres. Families with a parent or child who has a special need of this kind may qualify for assistance. An information sheet on special needs is available from the Holiday Care Service.

Some unions – NALGO, for example – have holiday centres and run holiday schemes for members and their families. Local union branches should be able to supply information.

Any application for financial assistance, whether made directly by a family, or by referral through a welfare agency, should contain as much detail as possible about the applicant's circumstances.

There is a large range of holiday guides on the market, catering for every interest at all prices.

Check what is available from your local library, and browse through the travel section at a bookshop to see which one best meets you requirements.

The Holiday Care Service particularly recommends the *'Where to Stay'* series of guides produced by the National Tourist Boards, and *'The Family Holiday Guide'* which has a good choice of family accommodation at budget prices.

During university and college vacations accommodation is available *(both self-catering, and with meals provided)* on many campuses. Further details are

available from –
BUAC (British Universities Accommodation Consortium) • Freepost • Box 937 • University Park Nottingham NG7 1BR   Telephone 0602 504571
and
HEAC (Higher Education Accommodation Consortium) 36 Collegiate Crescent • Sheffield S10 2BP
Telephone 0742 683759

You could also consider volunteering for one of the many projects from conservation to holidays for the disabled with organisations offering board and lodging – and sometimes help with transport.

Exchanging homes with a family from a different part of Britain or another part of the world solves the problem of leaving your house unattended while you are on holiday, and provides free accommodation when you get to your destination. For a fee – in the region of £20-35 – agents will put families in touch.

If you really cannot afford to holiday together, you may still want to be able to get some respite from the children while they have a good time. Holidays for children on their own are not always cheap, because of the need for supervisors and instructors, but they do answer a real need, especially for working parents during the long summer holidays.

Methods of transport
Coach
Coach is the cheapest way to travel, particularly for shorter distances. Details of services can be obtained from local bus stations or travel agents. National Express operates the most comprehensive

LONE PARENT SURVIVAL GUIDE

coach network in Britain. Details available from –

National Express
Victoria Coach Station • Buckingham Palace Road
London SW1W 9TP   Telephone 071 730 0202
Reductions for children vary between routes and services – 50-75% of the adult fare is usual.

Rail
The British Rail *'Family Railcard'* saves money on train fares, particularly for longer journeys, for large family groups, and if you are likely to use it more than once during the year for which it is valid. Either one or two adults *not necessarily related* can buy the *'Family Railcard'* for £26 at the time of going to press. They can then travel – with up to two other adults – for half the normal fare each, as long as between one and four children travel with them (the child fare is £1). Leaflets and application forms are available from most British Rail stations, travel centres, British Rail appointed agents and the Holiday Care Service.

Air
Airlines offer a wide range of discounted prices. Approach them direct for the best deals, or ask at you local travel agent. There are off-season reductions and *APEX* and *SUPER APEX* offer reductions for advance bookings. At the other end of the scale, last minute standby fares are heavily discounted, but rather risky at busy times of year. Charter flights and *'bucket shops'* may offer even cheaper flights. Book through reputable firms with ABTA or IATA affiliation. Make sure of firm bookings and valid

tickets before parting with your money.
The travel agent section of your local *Yellow Pages* directory will list many firms offering cut price air fares.

Holiday organisations in Britain
Several British organisations cater specifically for one-parent families' holidays, these are –

H.E.L.P. *(Holiday Endeavour for Lone Parents)*
29 The Crescent • Woodlands • Doncaster
South Yorkshire DN6 6PE   Telephone 0203 725315
A charity offering low cost caravan and chalet holidays for lone parents and their children. Early booking is essential. Send sae for details.

The Holiday Care Service
2 Old Bank Chambers • Station Road • Horley Surrey RH6 9HW   Telephone 0293 774535
A registered charity which provides support and information for people whose circumstances make access to holidays difficult. Free information sheets are available on a variety of holiday topics which will be of interest to one-parent families at different income levels.   Send an sae.

H.O.P. *(Holidays for One Parent Families)*
51 Hampshire Road • Droylsden • Manchester M35 7PH
Telephone 061 370 0337.
Arranges holidays and day trips at discount prices, brochure on application with sae.

SPLASH *(formerly Gingerbread Holidays)*
19 North Street • Plymouth PL4 9AH
Telephone 0752 674067
Has a wide ranging programme of holidays for one-parent families at concessionary rates which apply throughout the year. Special rates for holiday camps and for groups. Holidays for unaccompanied children during August. As a member of ABTA will negotiate discounts for holidays advertised by other ABTA firms. Runs a Savings Scheme to help save up for holidays. Also arranges holidays abroad – *see next section*.

Gingerbread
35 Wellington Street • London WC2 7BN
Telephone 071 240 0953
The London National office usually arrange a lone-parent holiday to include their Annual General

Meeting, for members. They will also supply addresses of local Gingerbread Groups, which may arrange holidays for one parent family members.

Holidays abroad
Organisations specialising in lone-parents' holidays abroad are –

One Parent Family Holidays
Kildonan Courtyard • Barrhill • Dirvan • South Ayrshire KA26 0PS   Telephone 0465 82288
Started in 1975 by lone parents to specialise in continental holidays for one-parent families. Some are expensive, some definitely in the 'budget' range, including short breaks abroad. They will advise individuals on specific holiday options if they send details of their requirements. Please send an sae with all enquiries.

SPLASH *(formerly Gingerbread Holidays)*
Address as above
Offers a wide choice of holidays abroad, including hotels, apartments, and caravan accommodation. Skiing holiday in most recent brochure. *(See also previous section)*. Please send an sae.

The Holiday Care Service
Address as above
Has information listing commercial tour operators who offer reductions for children accompanying one adult – rather than the usual reduction when two adults are travelling. Note that these concessions apply mainly outside the peak holiday season.

House Swaps
Home Base Holidays • 7 Park Avenue • London N13 SP9
Telephone 081 886 8752

Fee in 1993 is £32.00.

Working Holidays
British Trust for Conservation Volunteers
36 St Mary's Street • Wallingford • Oxon OX10 EU
Telephone 0491 39766

National Youth Agency
17-23 Albion Street • Leicester LE16GD
Telephone 0533 471200

Produces a leaflet entitled Voluntary Work and Young People, priced 50 pence.

Holidays for Children
Chidren's Country Holiday Fund
1st Floor (rear) • 42/43 Lower Marsh • Tanswell Street London SE1 7RG   *Telephone 071 928 6522*

A registered charity which organises camps and country holidays in private homes for London Children. Age range 5-12 *(boys up to 13)*. Children are mainly referred by social services or schools, but parents who apply direct can be put in touch with the appropriate contact in their area. Parents asked to make a small contribution to cost.

Forest School Camps
110 Burbage Road • London SE24 9HD

A long-established charity which takes children to camp. Age range 6-18. Camping holidays arranged to suit the age group involved. About 10 per cent of children are referred through welfare agencies. There are discretionary subsidies for families who cannot afford the full cost. Parents who volunteer to work as staff in camps may be eligible for reductions for their children. Concessionary rates increase for regular campers. Stamped addressed envelope please. Early booking essential.

SPLASH
Address as above
Arranges holidays for unaccompanied children, for example farm holidays *(for 6-9 year-olds);* holidays at a seaside activity centre *(for 8-12 year-olds);* canal boat cruises *(for 13-15 year-olds).* Please send an sae for brochure. Early booking essential.

Youth Hostels Association
Trevellyan Lodge • 8 St Stephen's Hill • St Albans Herts AL1 2DY   Telephone 0727 855215
Most of the YHA Adventure Holidays are geared to the 16-plus age group, but there are opportunities for 12-15 year-olds on sailing, canoeing, water sports, rock climbing and mountain craft and riding holidays. Special one-parent family membership available. Early booking is essential.

YMCA
640 Forest Road • London E17 3DZ
Telephone 081 520 5599
YMCA, a non-profit making charitable organisation, runs camps and day camp centres for children aged 5-14 in Kent, Middlesex and Cumbria.

LONE PARENT SURVIVAL GUIDE

USEFUL ORGANISATIONS

National Council for One Parent Families
255 Kentish Town Road • London NW5 2LZ
Telephone 071 267 1361
For expert information on all issues affecting lone parents and referrals to local help agencies.

Gingerbread
35 Wellington Street • London WC2E 7BN
Telephone 071 240 0953
For contacts with local groups around the country.

Scottish Council for Single Parents
13 Gayfield Square • Edinburgh EH1 3NX
Telephone 031 220 0929

Citizens Advice Bureaux (CAB)
Refer to local library or telephone directory
For advice on a wide range of practical problems.

Child Poverty Action Group
1-5 Bath Street • London EC1V 9PY
For welfare benefits advice.

DSS
Freephone 0800 666 555
For benefits information.

Money Advice Association
Aizlewoods Mill • Nursery Street • Sheffield S3 8GG
Telephone 0742 823165

For local money advice centres.

Law Centres Federation
Duchess House • 18-19 Warren Street • London W1P 5DB   *Telephone 071 387 8570*
For referrals to local law centres.

Women's Aid Federation
PO Box 391 • Bristol BS99 7WA

Telephone		
London	071 250 653337
Belfast	0232 249041
Bristol	0272 633494
Cardiff	0222 390874
Edinburgh	031 225 8011
Manchester	061 839 8574

For women who are suffering from domestic violence.

Shelter
88 Old Street • London EC1V 9AX
    Telephone 071 253 0202
For people in housing need.

Cruse
Cruse House • 126 Sheen Road • Richmond • Surrey TW9 1UR
Support groups around the country for bereaved people.

Association of Bereavement Services
68 Chalton Street • London NW1 1JR
    Telephone 071 247 0617

ESSENTIAL

Relate – Marriage Guidance
Herbert Gray College • Little Church Street • Rugby
Warwickshire CV21 3AP   Telephone 0788 573241

National Family Conciliation Centre
Shaftsbury Centre • Percy Street • Swindon • Wilts
SN2 2AZ   Telephone 0793 514055

Family Mediators Association
The Old House • Rectory Gardens • Henbury • Bristol
BS10 7AQ   Telephone 0272 500140

British Pregnancy Advisory Services
Austy Manor • Wooton Waven • Solihull B95 6BX
*   Telephone 0564 793225*

Brook Advisory Centres
153a East Street • London SE17 2SD
*   Telephone 071 708 1234*

Solicitors Family Law Association
The Administrative Sectetary • PO Box 302 • Keston
Kent BR2 6EZ   Telephone 0689 850227

National Council for Abducted Children
(RE-UNITE)
PO Box 4 • London WC1X 8XY   Telephone 071 404 8356